Present Vanishing

ALSO BY DICK ALLEN

The Day Before: New Poems (2003)
Ode to the Cold War: Poems New and Selected (1997)
Flight and Pursuit (1987)
Overnight in the Guest House of the Mystic (1984)
Regions with No Proper Names (1975)
Anon and Various Time Machine Poems (1971)

Present Vanishing

Dick Allen

Sarabande Books
LOUISVILLE, KENTUCKY

FIRST EDITION

Managing Editor
Sarabande Books, Inc.
2234 Dundee Road, Suite 200
Louisville, KY 40205

Library of Congress Cataloging-in-Publication Data

Allen, Dick, 1939–
    Present vanishing : poems / by Dick Allen. — 1st ed.
        p.   cm.
    ISBN 978-1-932511-64-2 (pbk. : alk. paper)
    I. Title.

    PS3551.L3922P74 2008
    811'.54—dc22   2007048857

ISBN-13: 978-1-932511-64-2

Cover image provided courtesy of the Associated Press

Cover and text design by Charles Casey Martin

Manufactured in Canada
This book is printed on acid-free paper.

Sarabande Books is a nonprofit literary organization.

THE KENTUCKY ARTS COUNCIL

The Kentucky Arts Council, a state agency in the Commerce Cabinet,
provides operational support funding for Sarabande Books with state
tax dollars and federal funding from the National Endowment for the
Arts, which believes that a great nation deserves great art.

for Lori, Rich, Tanya

Only when our minds stop racing, only when we allow ourselves to be in one place, can we truly be present in the here and now.

—Andrew Weiss, *Beginning Mindfulness*

When you and I met, the meeting was over very shortly, it was nothing. Now it is growing something as we remember it. But still we know very little about it. What it will be when I remember it as I lie down to die, what it makes in me all my days till then—that is the real meeting. The other is only the beginning of it.

—C. S. Lewis, *Out of the Silent Planet*

Brother Lawrence, a simple Christian saint, was out walking when he noticed a tree losing its leaves. This act, which he'd seen probably thousands of times before, sent him into a state of enlightenment. This is the Zen Mind: suddenly seeing something again for the first time.

—Daniel Levin, *The Zen Book*

Contents

Acknowledgments

Grateful acknowledgement is given to the editors and publishers of the following, in which some of these poems first appeared, a few in slightly different versions:

Agni: "At the Shrine of the Lost Cause"
Alimentum: "Choose What You Please"
American Poetry Review: "Quiet Wonder," "Rowing a Boat Across China"
Ascent: "Mid-December"
The Atlantic Monthly: "Five Statues of Buddha," "Private Grief"
Boulevard: "See the Pyramids Along the Nile," "The Table Before Me"
Connecticut Review: "The Gardener of West Hartford," "So, What Did You Do With Your Life?"
Edge City Review: "I Will Buy a Chicken"
Georgia Review: "We Talk Physics Into the Night"
The Gettysburg Review: "B&B," "Dada"
Hampden-Sydney Poetry Review: "Don't Tell Me There's No Hope"
The Hudson Review: "And All Shall Be Well; And All Shall Be Well;..." "A Cautionary," and "Humble Pie"
Inkwell: "Washing Each Other's Hands"
Margie: "Unrelenting Fear"
The Modern Review: "Listening to Kandinsky's Paintings," "Plum"
The New Criterion: "On Tenterhooks"
Newington-Cropsey Cultural Studies: Poetry: "Buttering the Bread"
North American Review: "The Dragons of America," "The Post-Surrealist"
Notre Dame Review: "The Saratoga Country Highway Department"

The Ontario Review: "All Those Years When Nothing Happened,"
                "The Blind"

Ploughshares: "The Fakirs"

Poetry: "The Adult Section," "High Horses"

Raritan: "Radiator Frog"

River City Review: "Elvis of Memphis"

The Seneca Review: "Vietnam Veterans Hospital"

The Southeast Review: "Crab Apples"

Tar River Poetry: "Pixels"

The Texas Review: "Mist"

Washington Square: "Hornets' Nests"

West Coast Review: "A Curse"

"B&B" was reprinted on *Enskyment*

"See the Pyramids Along the Nile" was reprinted in *The Best American Poetry 2006*.

"On Tenterhooks" and "We Talk Physics Into the Night" were reprinted on *Poetry Daily*.

"The Fakirs" and "So, What Did You Do With Your Life?" were reprinted in *Poetry Calendar 2006* and *Poetry Calendar 2007*.

"And All Shall Be Well; And All Shall Be Well; ..." was reprinted in *The Year's Best American Spiritual Writing: 2007*.

"*I am here to be here, like these rocks and sky and snow, like this hail that is falling down out of the sun.*"
—Peter Matthiessen, *The Snow Leopard*

GOAT

after Peter Matthiessen

This goat by the crooked door,
gazing through sheets of rain into the mud,
a cosmic vision? Or might it simply be
my grandfather's goat, the one I remember
from the barn in Saratoga on Congress Street,
the black and white goat that lived among the chickens
back in the darkness. "I long to let go,
drift free of things,
to accumulate less, depend on less,
to move more simply," the traveler in the Himalayas
said to the cosmic goat, yet I recall
that goat my grandfather named without imagination,
"Billy Goat,"
to which he used to croon,
"*Billy? Billy? Billy?*" and the goat
in all its stink and foolishness and hunger
would come to my grandfather's hand,
here to be here, here to look no further.

3

ALL THOSE YEARS WHEN NOTHING HAPPENED

All those years when nothing happened
the blind beggar was approaching you.
He was singing.
He was wiping his face with an orange bandanna.
And when he came to a lake a small boy would emerge from the reeds
to lead him around it.
And when he came to a city, feral cats
adopted him, and they led him safely from border to border.
And when he came to a highway
he raised both hands above his head and the traffic snarled
to let him cross. All those years
you were eating the remains of crow
as you sat on the back porch of a small gray house,
facing out over a clothesline and a meadow. You were almost nothing.
You did not have denim-blue eyes or sympathetic ears
or Bob Dylan's buggy-whip voice,
nor were you wearing anything that would remind anyone of computers,
but the blind beggar kept approaching you anyway
through sunflower fields and fields of Joe Pye Weed,
around rural junkyards, the wrecks piled upon each other
like segments of broken spine,
singing (he was always singing)
"Take the A Train," "Sentimental Journey," "Mama Loves Mambo,"
"Where Have all the Flowers Gone"
while you were at your ordinary job,

doing your ordinary job in your ordinary way,

counting the money, what money there was, if that's what you did,

as the small town—or was it a city—tumbled around you.

You felt, sometimes, as if you had somehow stepped into the wrong life,

a life of Quick-Marts, Doc-in-the-Boxes,

auto shopping lots on main highways leading out of town,

junk mail, junk cereal, junk TV, junk T-shirt slogans,

no loitering, no lingering, no lasting, no ever-lasting,

your life mainly snatches of TV skits,

and what you grabbed from the kitchen on the way from the bathroom,

what you would be trying to forget if you could remember,

while the blind beggar was approaching you. In his back pocket

he carried a first edition of Ginsberg's *Howl*

he would ask others to read to him when he stopped for the night.

He was tall, he was short, he was fat, he was thin

depending upon the seasons. He liked the feel of water glasses,

the sound of truck cement mixers slowly revolving,

contrasts of dirt roads and paved roads and pebble roads

beneath his feet. He liked the smell

of candle smoke and dusk, lilacs, deep green leaves,

water and willows and the way the sky smelled

as he emerged into it from a long climb up through a tenement

onto the roof, into warm circles of sunlight.

He liked to run both hands across the hoods of cooling cars,

and the shoulders of anyone, feeling bones and muscles,

but even doing these things he thought of you always,

knowing you were waiting for him although you did not quite know

    you were waiting,

that sometimes you could almost see him down the road, the speck of him,

or hear his songs at night, from so long a ways off

they seemed to be the songs of mother and child, moles and spiders,

tiny computer chips—the blind beggar

who was bringing you the present you had always wanted,

a bowl of blueberries, maybe,

to sit out in the sun and eat from a bowl of blueberries

while the blind beggar sang, perhaps

"Alice's Restaurant," every verse,

and you saw him at last: his onyx ring,

the shades of gray in his pepper and salt beard,

his American smile, or Italian, or African, or Chinese, or Colombian,

the admiration of your wife or husband or your closest friend,

his strangeness you had been missing for so long

   that your whole body never quite felt rhymed,

his vividness, his god-damned / god-blessed vividness,

how he listened intently to every true thing you said,

like "carrots"

or "Sweet Virginia hills,"

as you learned to say true things again,

his hands cupping his chin, leaning his whole self toward you,

requesting you simply,

"Tell me of you and your world."

RADIATOR FROG

Dark green, a wet dark mossy green,
the dark green of summer leaf clusters
just before a storm comes in from the Appalachians,
            you, radiator frog,
your look cousin to the owl's look: all bulbous eyes
            and quivering mouth,
now as you squat on our unpainted kitchen radiator
like the clogged soul of a green rock
lifted from some dark corner of the Monagahelia,
your bumpy back a wet green crumpled washcloth,
haunches covering your spindly legs—you,
globular-throated creature of green swamps,
clenched fist of spray-painted cement,
never to leap, but always poised to leap
like the ugly human sayings of *I always meant to,*
I never quite could get my courage up—
inert brain, lump of possibilities,
may warmth seep through you, steam surround you,
flies in ointment and the jellied tongue
bless this house you'll augur all the winter long.

MIST

Photographers love it, how it blurs a background
so a fisherman or stone or single cypress branch
highlighted against it

is all the more detailed. Smoke obscures, but mist
is a promise of lifting,
bride's face emerging from the bridal veil,

or in Japanese movies,
the first horse nudging from a misty forest
and then the vast army. Scientists

know it as a fine array of water droplets
suspended between heaven and the earth;
the drunkard sees it form above cracked ice,

the grocer as a spray to cool his vegetables.
And in its role of all that is to come
it may be perfume

hovering about a woman's neck. Most beautiful
when windowed by a spray of sun
and rainbows arch from it; most frightening

when lurking on the Baskerville's dark moors,
the mist is everything not quite itself
that touches and is touched—that lack

of willfulness, that lace, that gossamer
impossibly romantic as poetic lives;
that present of the present vanishing

and here at once: a swirl of white
floating on dark ocean waves, the thought we'd lost
discovered shipwrecked in a shoal of clouds.

AMERICAN BUDDHISM

I.

Five Household Statues of Buddha

The bronze Buddha in our living room,
his eyes closed, his hands resting comfortably
against his inside thighs,
what does he mean to tell me about the river heron?

And the green sleeping Buddha
stretched out upon his side along our poetry bookcase,
serene as a watch fob in his stylized pose,
what is he saying about the price of all good things?

What is the black Buddha asking,
sitting on the mantelpiece
as if on a lotus? *If you would not suffer,*
you must not desire?

And the small Tara Buddha
who looks upon the road outside
from the windowsill perch she shares with both our cats,
is she so content I cannot learn from her?

Lastly, the happiness Buddha,
late of China, his round gold stomach glistening

under my fading light,

shall I not trust him to laugh my life into his?

II.

"Entering the Monastery, We Give Up Nothing"

Just because the dust is full of gods
and what red and green have in common can't be put into words,
doesn't mean you should stop opening the newspaper
or jogging backward every Wednesday. Just because
when asked who we are, we say who we were,
and the universe is really a small delicatessen,
is no reason to run off to Bristol, Connecticut
with a chip on your shoulder. You have a duty
to the unchopped liver, the unmade bed, the bookshelves
all out of order—a duty
you must fulfill with grace and courtesy
and great daily attention to the sacredness of things.
So just because
they found jewels in the ashes of that one proclaimed to be a buddha
doesn't mean you shall not march against the war,
or teach what little you know to those who know too much,
and curse in midtown traffic, wondering
why the light is always changing right before your eyes.

III.

Quiet Wonder

In Chinese landscape paintings, the scroll ones,
where you carefully uncover, right to left, a forest
and walk through it slowly, all your attention on edge,
listening to the wind, which may be a dragon's breathing
or the simple susurration of old pines,
there comes upon you what the Chinese sages called
"Quiet Wonder." It can only be evoked, they said,
never commanded. Go down a certain path
and you'll reach a fishing village beside a river
that's only a turbulence of lines
on which a boat rests. The village itself
is several more lines, a triangular roof,
a window suggestion. Is no one at home? A few turns further,
and there's the bridge that everyone has walked across,
a crow that everyone has seen. Hands on the railing,
you listen to the crow, your eyes
catching in all this sepia that sudden flash of red
you know must be a single poppy
placed exactly there to draw you on
or rather into. *How far away*
we are from computers here, and cell phones,
and television cameras panning over everything! And now
the rice fields stretch out for a thousand miles
and the bluish mountains, and all this white autumn sky.

IV.

At the Shrine of the Lost Cause

You must put a *sandaru* on your head,
as in the Zen koan. You must walk into moonlight,
feeling the moonlight as if it were the wind caught sleeping,
twisted around a lamp post. When everything's awful,
you must be good to strangers.
More than you know, their luggage needs your hands.
You must express yourself truly,
although you may stammer when you reach the participles.
In the pure silliness of the name "Juicy Fruit Gum,"
or your fingertip's feeling of buttons
like tiny rabbits going into buttonholes,
you must exult. *Sing a song of six pence, a pocket full of rye.*
The only way out of all your obligations
is in your own mind. There, on that small main street,
you must saunter along, kicking a stone
until you're tired of it and wish it lost,
then pick it up and fling it into a used car lot.
At last you can laugh and get yourself a milkshake.
Or if all else seems dust, you must right now
listen to your breathing for several minutes,
the inrush of air, the outrush of air,
all that keeps you alive invisible but you can feel it
and you hold a key and the glory is it fits nothing
or perhaps there's a statue, serene, without expression,
or maybe a tall bamboo door.

V.

Rowing a Boat Across China

It's not an easy task. The oarlocks rust,
the crows seem too overhead.
Once, as we neared a village under a steep cliff,
oxen blocked our way for many hours,
lily pads grew enormous and almost engulfed us
but our craft proved worthy. We placed below the gunwales
the *Analects,* a dog-eared copy of the *Tao*
and a foot-high Buddha statue,
which doubled as both incense burner and anchor. Such a journey!
You'll never know how much our bodies ached,
our brows sweated. I saw two dragons
in that quadrant of the sky no one's yet mapped
and we heard constant temple bells. Lin-chi wrote,
"When you meet a master swordsman,
Show him your sword.
When you meet a man who is not a poet,
do not show him your poem."
But many showed us their poems, so many,
sometimes I began to think the world floated on poems
or at least scattered verses. Toward Fall,
we rowed for many miles of deepest wonder
through a carpet of floating leaves,
sighing and singing. At last we'd learned
to be at home in any place,
no matter how squalid or how beautiful.

As with a room, so with a life:
to look at one corner and realize the other three.
When the first snows came,
we floated into an odd region of deep pines
where shapes stood on the water like warriors in stone.
Our oars broke the ice skim of an oblong lake
to leave dark buttons on a white silk blouse
and snow fell on the backs of our necks, melting into our robes.
Such coldness! So many views, always changing:
a Shar-pei running on the banks, a hillside shrine,
peasants carrying toward us bowls of steaming rice.

VI.

Mid-December

Sometime about now
would be a good time to reinvent serious mazurka
and the way shirts unbutton. You could ask yourself,
"Why don't I just get sick?"
or go out walking through a great windy forest. About now
you might want to empty your pockets
of all those Chinese fortunes you've been carrying,
and remember there's nothing but mystery in the world,
although it hides itself behind the fabric of each day,
shining brightly, and we don't even know it.
Since this is mid-December, you might wish to celebrate
pomegranates, antique automobiles.

You might wish to drive to an unfamiliar town
and walk its streets, humming *"Sha-na-na-na. Sha-na-na-na"*
while you look at wreaths on churchyard graves. In mid-December
the streams and rivers run so slowly
they seem to be seventeenth-century sermons or adagios
and the snow waits furiously behind the sky's metallic sheen.
So you might want to rid yourself of excess caution
and eat figgy pudding, and dance in the old courtyard,
for whole trees are swaying,
and the wilds of your life are your own.

PLUM

You can make a plum in one brushstroke, or two,
and if you're skilled enough,
you can leave a small area of white paper to one side,
suggesting a highlight,
says my Chinese watercolor book. It's best
if you start with a heavy brush or a heavy heart,
a daydream or nightmare. Most important,
you should always plan for fly specks, splatters, a telephone call
right in the middle of a stem or blossom—
that something going wrong that you can change to right
with acceptance and calm. Keep the Four Gems
forever close to you: brush and paper,
inkstone and inkstick. And learn the rules,
study them, use them, break them—in that order
should you wish to progress. The plum
is a beautiful thing
with all sorts of shading in a skin so close to bruising
it seems like late summer,
but to truly possess it, you must not desire it,
nor copy it down exactly, says my book— ·
which includes many pictures, not only of plums
but of dicentras, orange climbers,
windblown and rainswept bamboo.

To study Buddhism is to study the self.
To study the self is to forget the self.
To forget the self is to be one with others.

  —Dogen

Who we are at the most intimate and direct level can never
be fixed. Essentially, individual form is an ever-changing
aggregation of elements—world and self interacting with
each other in the continuous activity of co-creation. Making
a portrait of the Buddha or anyone else is to make visibly
and palpably, the flow of interdependent existence.

  —Lindy Lee (Australian painter),
  in Buddha: Radiant Awakening

LISTENING TO KANDINSKY'S PAINTINGS

I come late to such music: the yellow trumpets,
the double bass of the blue;
from red, the tuba and from white, the silence,
and here and there the circular black note,
no future, no hope,
floating in these seas of sticks and stones;
and I come late to the indigo concertos,
those little pale rhapsodies of ivory zigzags
drifting as if unconducted,
the green chords, adagios of wavering altos,
and whole orchestral fields
beneath his baton. I walk over halos,
I take the long screech of an elevator
up to pyramids of hope,
the petits fours, the marzipans
of shading and nuance, popsicle dancers,
bent tusks and unicorn horns;
and I step out
onto a platform of musicians' hats,
cones and triangles, spheres and inner worlds,
reincarnated,
to listen to that isosceles on the corner,
that blur of pink calling me

from a pool of orange inside a pit of gray,
you were too literal,
and lived your life as if it held no sound.

THE ADULT SECTION

When I was eleven and the librarian finally let me in to browse alone,

showing me where the light switches were for each stack

and teaching me a few things about call numbers,

at first I walked on tiptoe, afraid

those huge stern books, in their huge stern leather bindings,

The Collected Works of Horace Walpole, for instance,

and *The English Poets: Selections,*

with Critical Introductions by Various Writers

and a General Introduction by Matthew Arnold,

edited by Thomas Humphrey, M.A.,

Late Fellow of Brasenose College, Oxford,

were going to tumble over onto me

and literally kill me with the weight of their knowledge,

especially *The Proceedings of the New York State Geographical Society,*

in its fifteen gigantic volumes up to 1947,

each big enough to crush two babies with one blow,

and complete in one volume apiece *The Works* of Byron and Tennyson

with plentiful illustrations—books so heavy you had to deal with them

as if you were lifting a small boulder from an English brook,

walking them spread-kneed to the round mahogany reading table,

which was four times the size of any dining room table I'd ever seen,

and ten times as imposing, especially if some adult sat ghastly there.

Then you'd heave the books up under one of the six reading table lamps,

beneath which dangled straight down

tarnished bronze chain cords. I should add, for the pleasure of the image, that whoever, long ago, had replaced the original oil lamps,

had ordered the chains much too long, so that each excess lay in a puddle,

like the coils of an Indian fakir's rope trick.... Alone,

at eleven years old, in the adult section of the Round Lake Public Library,

I first began to feel all those strange names floating around me in the
    semi-dark,

all those angels, will of the wisps, great swooping birds, doves,

ravens, raptors: *Kant, Hegel, Saintsbury, Schopenhauer,*

Catallus, Swedenborg, Pliny the Elder,

Cervantes, Alexis de Tocqueville, Willa Cather,

St. Augustine, Seneca, Toynbee, Charlotte Brontë

Racine, Stendahl, Goethe, Dostoevsky,

and I knew what they said about old library books was true.

        They whisper,

seek wisdom, seek wisdom, seek wisdom, seek wisdom, seek wisdom

repeated so often the words begin to ebb and flow inside you,

compelling you to read until your eyes fall out.... The librarian,

a kind elderly woman who wore her glasses on a chain

as librarians did then, long before it became the fashion,

would call me out of the stacks, or away from that reading table

ten minutes before closing time, and I'd emerge

blinking under the arabesque light of the small chandelier,

to stand before the checkout desk, lugging six volumes—the limit

for children allowed in the adult section—

and *"Are you sure you can handle this?"* she'd murmur,

hefting a Plato's *Republic* or *Plays* by Oliver Goldsmith,

or *Lysistrada* (that one I snuck past her!)

to which I'd say, *"I think so, ma'am,"* being at that time

24

under the common illusion that librarians, especially elderly ones,

had read—as part of their job—every single book in the library.

At last the stamp would go *stamp stamp* six times,

sometimes her wrist slightly rocking

if she'd clobbered the take out slip too lightly at first,

and I'd be out the door, walking slowly,

past the gargoyle fountain, under the huge old pines,

frightened, elated, sometimes trembling,

sure that the weight of the world had come into my arms,

ready to learn what it was that I should do.

DADA

Dada spread his fingers on a cloud of nails
inching across the eyes of several tourists
come to gawk at New York. Dada said
keep your thoughts on how a train derails
and angels love tunnels. On Dada's wrists,
lips turned into mirrors and loaves of bread
leaned from the doorways, raggletails
ending their stories. Dada in the harbor mist
never wore a rainbow on his head.
Say that for him. But Dada never stalked
slowly though a pine forest, or climbed the stairs
over a sleeping dog, and when my prayers
nudged his shoulder, Dada only chalked
narwhals on the backs of my kid gloves,
elephants on stars. Still, still I loved
to pull his beard and follow his jaywalk.

"CHOOSE WHAT YOU PLEASE"

"Choose what you please," the waiter offered,
in the ultra-costly, once-in-a-lifetime Boston restaurant,
as he wheeled his cart of pastries from the kitchen door:
cannoli, napoleons, bismarcks,
and some concoction so whipped cream and chocolate,
I swear it levitated from its silver platter.
"But only one," said my mother,
who'd been so nervous through the meal she barely spoke,
the expense, the thought of the expense,
quite beyond her. But my father,
so proud of his book contract even his eyeballs glimmered
above the whitest tablecloth I'd ever laid my hands upon,
whispered, "I don't know which likes me most,
unless it's this beauty." He pointed
and the biggest, most delicious-looking, most superior, most supreme,
pastry of pastries
got lifted onto his dessert plate. I blinked at the platter's void,
as all the other pastries seemed to cringe
or turn into molasses. "Well, Doris? Well, Dickie?"
he asked. My mother, with a small shake of her head,
declined, and I
trying to follow her lead, picked the only confection
remotely modest—something with berries, I think,
in a sweet cup of dough,
trying to please not only it, but her

27

who cared so much for appearances she seldom left our house
afraid *they,* meaning the world, meaning even the pigeons of the world,
would judge her to have failed
for having hoarded money only to have it flung away,
into this or that shame. *Have I pleased the things I've chosen*
enough to be worthy of them,
enough for them to fall apart the moment
my fork touches their crust,
enough to have them melt inside my mouth,
as my father said his pastry did?...
as he paid the bill, leaving a huge fat tip conspicuously placed
upon his dessert plate, the dollars sticking to the crumbs.
Is my house pleased with me? My Japanese pen? My computer?
Every mood I drive into myself? I was watching
my mother's mouth downturn until she faked a smile
at the maître d', the coat check girl, the doorman
who didn't care if she pleased him, not at all,
sad, sad woman, on that sad, sad day it was.

ELVIS OF MEMPHIS

combs his hair
doesn't want to go nowhere

eats peanut butter and banana sandwiches
twitches

is seized with a sudden need to play the fifth chord
what toward?

sits on a boulder by the Mississippi
looking pretty

waiting for his voice to change
how strange

that from a green apple bin
the gods shall choose him

Elvis
of Memphis

troubadour, paramour, saboteur,
movie star

in the someplace ahead
where the mist is rising from magnolia beds

and a new black Cadillac careens
down Beale Street past the Laundromat machines

empty now
because it's only morning anyhow

...and won't it be something, won't it be nice
won't that boy have a life.

THE SARATOGA COUNTY HIGHWAY DEPARTMENT

Two hours of work each day. The rest of it
coffee and jokes. Large moths meandered above us,
come in from dusty staircases and stairwells
to their dubious daytime home beneath the 1890s skylight. One employee
at the far right drafting table who moved nothing but his shoulders
would say, *"I don't know about that. I don't know"*
to whoever approached him. Another,
head buried in his arms, green visor poking up like a cowlick,
twitched in his sleep as if experiencing silverfish.
A third, the one who guarded the door,
would go into a mania of papers-in-manila-folders sorting
whenever the ancient boss, left over from the days of patronage,
stared moodily in. For a moment after the boss left,
the clerk would sort wildly in place, then collapse,
leaning as far backward in his swivel chair as balance would let him.
With eyes closed, he'd say, *"Whew, that was a doozy"*
and mean it. He was one of those people
who always mean everything they say, nothing more, nothing less,
the kind you're forced to listen to on bus stop lines, who are
absolutely sure the world is literal.... In the Saratoga County Highway
    Department
what we did was send out survey teams, plan new roads,
analyze soil, and re-evaluate bridges,
all of which sounds so utterly important in life,

31

it amazes me now that none of our work got completed,
and that nobody cared. *The chances, the opportunities, the glories*
life has to offer! The splendors!... All of us were entitled,
even me, the lowest of the low, the summer office help
who alternated Salems with Marlboros with Winstons down to their filters,
as I learned to draw the soil analysis charts in Indian ink
(*the wonderful richness of Indian ink, shining in its little Aladdin bottles!*)
bored out of my skull, the butt of all those failed jokes.

THE GARDENER OF WEST HARTFORD

Rather than the next election,
a house full of money, another European war,
he spent the entire morning thinking about blue roses,
the taste of blue rose hip jelly, the smell of blue rose attar,
floribundas, grandifloras, polyanthas,
trellises, fences, rugosas,
miniature blue roses with flowers no larger than a nickel,
and how the plot for a rose garden
should be protected from cold wind and open to sunlight,
surrounded by several cherub angel statues—and have read to it
at least one poem every day,
at sunset, preferably,
as a Tibetan master might calmly read instructions
to one who has died,
guiding the soul through great terror,
but then he lost focus,
feeling it all swirl in again: the rainforests,
fidelity and surety, the daily this and that
(there is no hope but we will have no fear)
and the blue roses faded, they turned to lavender
summer-and-autumns, mosses, hybrid teas.

UNRELENTING FEAR

I keep being hounded by that image of Larry Levis
on the Ohio Poetry Circuit,
not wanting to do anything but read and write
as the shadows come around him,
and that lonely Holiday Inn out on Interstate 70,
the rooms with their tolerable paintings,
where Levis, drug-worn,
holds a small orange notebook as he paces and sets on blue lines
his last terrible fragments,
and how, twenty miles away, in New Concord, Ohio,
(birthplace of John Glenn),
everything's what it should be on an autumn night,
the supper good, the television good, the sex good,
America so contented with how it is in the late 1980s,
who'd long for elsewhere. But Levis keeps thinking
What is it? What is it?
as he places in his notebook . . .
fire,
a child's head,
from somewhere irresolute, magnolias,
and a half-dozen thumbtacks lying on their sides.
Thought's needles and pins, he says aloud,
the doors of a stranger. He remembers
the moon above New Concord through the elms
and something his host had said, after the reading,

34

about a river of poets that flowed through here,

all nodding and bobbing,

amusing, amused

(through New Concord, Ohio,

birthplace of John Glenn),

and now Levis is angry

at all he's done to himself and others,

most of his life gone up in imaginings,

the life of a poet, goddamn it, goddamn your eyes,

then wouldn't you know it,

it's raining outside. Through the window,

incredible streaks of rain divide the night

while out on the Interstate,

the high-beams flick to life the road that vanishes

east to West Virginia, west to God knows where.

WE TALK PHYSICS INTO THE NIGHT

"Nothing is finished," Ye Feng says. "We're going after nothing,
bending its wavelengths, breaking across its borders
as if it were something one hangs out to dry
or beats with a paddle. It's like Zen," he says,
"so filled with paradoxes that it jumps through hoops
that aren't even there." He sighs,
his fifth beer going flat. At twenty-nine,
Ye Feng already knows his life is flying into particles,
antisite disorders, temperature dependencies,
superparamagnetic clusters with at least two sizes of moments
but no heavy-fermion behavior. "It's all optics," he says,
"or our Great Wall of China, which often isn't present
even when you're walking it." Beijing,
the black and white cat my wife and I have named
in honor of the birth city of the Fengs,
has utterly disappeared into the basement
or a black hole. On the mantelpiece,
the green and silver clock chimes two a.m.—another
twist of perception: how very late at night it's also early morning
and vice versa. "Minneapolis," says Ye Feng.
"My company's moving me to Minneapolis."
Outside the open window behind the couch,
a slight wind lazes through the dark, its passing
marked only by reactions of red maple leaves
and the soft tilting of grass and weeds. It's nothing,

36

we say—at this late or early hour too tired or drunk
to be conscious of sounding clever—a shoulder
on the higher binding energy side of the main peak,
a local moment. How pretentious we sound,
even to ourselves, how arrogant, how sincere!

THE POST-SURREALIST

When he learned about Gérard de Nerval
leading a lobster around the Jardin du Luxembourg
at the end of a blue ribbon
he began placing lobsters everywhere:
a Sears Tire Center,
at the end of a sentence concerning cheesecake,
in several women's basketball team photographs.
Once he set two lobsters
out in the desert where they could die a good death.
Lobsters, he declared,
are why we distrust maps. Lobsters are like red foxes,
they take over a room—chairs, tables, God help us.
Having no microchips in their stomachs,
they're free to wander the imagination
in a manner Wallace Stevens never dreamed possible.
Do lobsters play tennis?
Is the son of a lob, a lobster?
It's lobsters that make the world go round.
Lobster this, lobster that, lobster bisque.
Beware lobsters in high places.
A lobster a day keeps the doctor away.
Once in a blue lobster.
And the lobster of the Past, burnishing a branding iron,
humming "Blow the Man Down."
"I've never seen a lobster I didn't like,"

he told us, looking out to sea.
"It's their calm I appreciate, the way they scuttle
out of harm's way, and plan nothing,
how without them everything seems too unclawed, too straight ahead."
Had it succeeded, the Republic of Greenwich Village
would have declared the lobster as its mascot, he continued,
changing its motto from "Art, love, beauty and cigarettes"
to "Art, love, beauty and lobsters"
at the end of a blue ribbon,
strolling around, looking for all the world
like something meaningful if only you could find it.

THE DRAGONS OF AMERICA

Not the Ku Klux Klanners, may they burn in hell,
but the real dragons, fire-breathing, scaly-tailed,
nerve-wracking, hero-roasting, vulnerable-under-the-chin dragons
who live on horizons. Minnesota dragons, for instance,
slithering around the Mall of America on quiet nights,
seen only by security guards shining their flashlights into store front windows,
and the New York City dragons who skulk the tops of engine company roofs,
growling "Maria, Maria" rhythmically in not-bad baritones,
even the dragons seen by suburbanites dressed in brand-name leisureware
when the TV set goes dark and the dishwasher stops running:
window dragons, small but still ferocious as mad Chihuahuas,
usually Chinese red but here and there medieval green,
descended from the one whose fangs punctured Beowulf,
immigrated here, somehow bypassing Ellis Island,
looking in, always looking in and judging.... *Dragons on drag strips.*
Dragons in drag.... I sometimes wonder
what I should do if I meet one on the road,
some county highway of Kansas or New Mexico,
so deserted it lacks even a fruit stand?
Should I offer it a fair maiden or a frightened high school,
or a Hershey's chocolate bar or a bowl of chili?
"No, just admire it," dragon-hunters tell me. "They like to be admired.
They're quite exhibitionistic, like nudists and New Jersey politicians,
and if it seems upset, a Jorie Graham poem or two
has been known to calm one down and send another scurrying,

but you could also try vanilla wafers." American dragons,
they go on to say, have never lived in caves, preferring instead
the abandoned two-car garages of rural Vermont
or those kind of old factories where B–movies are filmed
—science fiction or gangster or most likely horror—
the movies with all those open corridors and metal cages and levels,
things to fall from that go *clang*.... Also, if you're brave or desperate,
two qualities pretty much the same when you think about them,
you might seek out dragon nests. What treasures
these dragons guard there! Marilyn Monroe calendars,
Captain Midnight decoders, a first edition of *Tamberlain,*
a peace pipe Custer supposedly smoked inside a Sioux tepee,
George Washington's slippers,
computer chips from Apollo, Elvis Presley peanut butter jars,
and the secret for creating rainfalls on demand. *Puff, the magic dragon
lived all alone....* I saw my first and only fire-breather
on a windy hilltop when I was driving across North Dakota,
waging my personal war with the American sense of humor
which undercuts everything serious for good or evil,
the funny undercutting the sad; the sad, the funny.
Even from far away the dragon was impressive,
the way it arched its back and its tail sent boulders flying.
How ugly it was, more ugly than any dying strip mall!
I thought I was dreaming it. But when I shut my eyes
and opened them again, the dragon was still there,
undulating, breathing out smoke and flame,
so I stopped. I got out of the car,
and took digital pictures—as one does when coming across

a UFO or a spectacular Coca-Cola bottle and case display,
like that huge rectangle erected outside an all-nite supermarket
to make a representation of the American flag,
we saw in Modesto, California, the evening of 9/11.

And wept.... *Young, young, we were young.*

Dragon tongue.

This is my song. Now I have sung.

More pictures
until the dragon moved off, leaving a golden sunset
and the scent of burning fields, maybe a trace of gunpowder.
"I've been fortunate," I said aloud. "I *have* been fortunate,"
and imagined it was because I'd lived before that time soon to arrive
when Americans will wake to see thousands of hillside dragons,
gathering, watching from the horizon, rubbing their claws together....
And I even half knew that when I tried to print out evidence
nothing would be there but that hilltop,
the golden sky behind it, a few low American clouds
that look like Conestoga wagons or white stallions
leisurely following each other, east to west to far west.

PRIVATE GRIEF

He was inducted out of God knows where,
and sent marching up and down the parade grounds blindfolded.

At night, in the barracks, he wept
into the dark of snoring men.

He looked like a fever, or some ragweed touched by sun,
or an elm with dark eyes.

Mail call found him sitting beside the flagpole,
cleaning his fingernails.

If you crossed him, he would cross you back
and mean nothing by it.

Where he went on leave was a secret
having something to do with pinewoods and racing cars.

He had no real appetite
except for potatoes, which he'd always fiercely hated.

The firing range fascinated him,
all that kneeling, all those silent targets.

When we sent him to war, he went without complaint
but came home no hero.

Private Grief, Private Grief, what are we to do with you?
"Ask me no questions and I'll tell you no lies."

Mustered out, he stepped into a barroom brawl,
then stepped back, unsmiling.

Private Grief, Private Grief,
I'll never believe you fought with all your heart.

Nobody really knows where the word "curse" came from. We can trace it back to the Anglo-Saxon "curs," but its origins beyond that are obscure, and cognates are unknown. In Anglo-Saxon, however, the meaning is quite clear. A "curs" is an imprecatory prayer or malediction. The idea of a "curse" in modern times is akin to hex, but the primary meaning of the word is the prayer or calling itself.

—The Free Online Dictionary

The message is clear: Food and drink will not satisfy the unfulfilled needs...desperate longing for inexhaustible abundance is very common in the Western psyche....

—Mark Epstein, *Thoughts Without a Thinker*

IN PROFILE

Think of me as always seen from the side,
never head on,
in profile, always having something else to hide,
or to abandon.

Think of me as always looking away,
only half here,
as the other side of the coin you could not see
or make appear.

Think of me as always facing left or right,
like a book page,
sometimes lingered on, more often flipped from sight,
leaving only this edge.

THE BLIND

Over days, we carefully made our blind out of old branches
slightly woven together and covered with fallen leaves,
so that inside—where we sat holding thermoses
filled with coffee brewed in dark kitchens,
no cream, no sugar, simply bitterness—
the sunlight, when it came with dawn,
was terribly mottled. Specks of sunlight moved back and forth
across our boots like large yellow insects
as we waited under the wind, holding our breath, listening
for the first lonely cries to come across the lake.
Then we'd rise out of what would seem nothing,
aim and fire and bring down from the heavens
those dead or wounded we might send the dog to fetch
or row out to ourselves, skirting the decoys we'd set
floating upon the waters in those early hours.
There, we kept our silence, not looking at each other,
or if we did, seeing no more than our young man faces,
tired and grim, so filled with misunderstandings,
doubt and guilt, no one would have believed
we'd come here by choice, and would return
year after year as long as the wretched blind
prevailed and the guns fit into our shoulders.

VIETNAM VETERANS HOSPITAL

Glass break in me, glass break, and in the fire
may some long train emerge
that I may vanish into rust and smoke. Glass break,
and gonging of ceramic bells. Two men
who thought that they were one come out of dust
and carry napalm like it was a child
of broken glass. Glass break. Collapse the sun
into many thimbles, drink from them. Page books
until larks fly from every noun and verb,
and hold your hand along the spine because
glass breaks and madrigals take root
in stony places.... Chant. Chant long
for monks in heather robes who kneel
beside a slum-faced boy, a girl
on such a farm no rainbow's found it yet,
but will. Hope God. Footprint His footprint. Seek
to understand the panic of a ledge,
why gardens float and skies of heron blue
darken into women's gowns. Strike mist
as if a feather-painted wall
where bicycles and oxen weave across rice plains
is waiting there.... I taste
the peach of Saigon afternoons, the apricot
of helicopter blades. Glass break. Glass break in me,

this ward is made from locust leaves and hair,
lost bone, lost minds
we buried in the valley of Lon Tron.

HIGH HORSES

Way up there, so high and well fed
they seem to be gods
or at least ridden by gods,
the high horses walk—so well bred

little disturbs them. Sedately,
they show off their steps,
canter right, canter left...perhaps
a brief trot, the perfect lifting of one knee

after another, and then
that exquisite gallop, that arrogance
of the totally convinced,
that disdain.... Then down

off the high horses
come their riders at last,
little men of the past,
clad in bright silken colors.

HORNETS' NESTS

Hundreds of them, accursed, their papery gray masses
hidden in eaves, in the junctures of two-by-fours,
or hanging in shrubs or behind olive branch foliage,
wait to be opened. Even long-abandoned nests,
those which turn immediately to ash at the poke of a broomstick,
threaten revenge. Inside their hexagram cells,
everything seems quivering, thrumming, as if the workers know
death will come at first frost—each worker's venom gone to waste
unless he can attack, protecting his basketball-sized empire.
And at the heart of everything, the larger body of sorrow
that will not die unless, from far away in the shadows,
we fill her nest with poison spray, or knock it down,
battering it, torching it when it falls, so that in some holy tomorrow
we may walk, unmolested, over the great green pastures.

THE FAKIRS

Cobras rise out of raw pits for them,
coils swaying
below each diamond head and red forked tongue.

When in old robes
they walk across a bed of sin, steam hisses
as if each footstep held a pod of water,

and to the murmurs of the crowd, they lift their feet
unscathed, and grin.
And sometimes they fast for days and sometimes they read minds

or pull iron spikes of pity from unbloodied palms.
But in their heart of hearts, their mind of minds
they know they are fakirs,

the secrets of the universe not theirs,
only illusions, only the herbal potions
passed down from their fathers. So, devoutly,

they pray for real magic, for their voices
to speak the miracles of gods
that they might truly float or cease to breathe

and then with one short gasp recover breath: the fakirs
with their snakes and their coals and their poetic phrases,
swarming the banks of our times.

A CURSE

We will not toss a fig to, nor remember
The thieving CEO, the slipshod builder,
Dope-pusher, crack-smoker, Mafia mobster.
We want to hear their names no more.

The crooked baseball player, the counterfeiter,
The general who would take no prisoner,
The playground bully, the child molester,
We want to hear their names no more.

Smudges on the landscape, insects in dogs' fur,
The drunken driver, the occasional wife beater,
The sniper crawling out from under God knows where,
We want to hear their names no more.

Mad or not, the serial axe-murderer,
The airplane hijacker, the suicide bomber,
Who cares what sad lost shapes their childhoods were?
We want to hear their names no more.

Let them be swept up by some janitor
And never mentioned in a single prayer.
Let every feature of them disappear.
We want to hear their names no more.

For they are dung and spit and gelatin and scar,
The dribble soaked into a chewed cigar,
Old knots in dirty hair, crepuscular.
We want to hear their names no more.

WASHING EACH OTHER'S HANDS

We do this slowly, we've practiced this so long,
looking for all the world like the M.C. Escher print
where the two hands draw each other drawing each other.
We lave our carpals, phalanges, metacarpals,
lifelines, heartlines, the anatomical snuffbox,
sometimes resentfully, sometimes with great joy,
each bar of soap between us slipping back and forth
in the hot sudsy water—*Dove, Crest, Lifebuoy, Ivory,*
sometimes one of those little round perfumed cakes
taken from a French hotel. In this together,
we lace and steeple, thumb a ride, slap palms for luck,
until dirt vanishes, troubles float away. We have no sins,
rinsing, exclaiming, exulting, excluding
all other hands that want to come on board.

THE TABLE BEFORE ME

In the presence of my enemies, this table,
   these grapes so purple they seem about to explode into heaven,
this whole wheat bread, these wedges of Edam,
   Fontina, Port Salut, Jarlsburg,
the pig with the apple in its mouth, juices searing its belly,
   yams, pineapples, petits fours, Spanish cremes,
I could go on and on. Certainly
   there are enemies in the shadows,
crude hoaxes and plots, grace notes gone bitter,
   but we shall deal with them another day.
For now, let the hair be anointed,
   the cup runneth over. Let music
pour from gigantic loudspeakers, an eclectic mix
   of Dixie Chicks and London Philharmonic,
some Gillespie for luck. Hang up more paintings,
   They shall be mainly blue sky with little figures
working the fields,
   and morning cityscapes, the laundry laughing,
pigeons flying up in great gusts from alleyways,
   a half-naked woman in a yellow dress. On the table before me
let lobster bisque steam, the shrimp alfredo
   wait with such joy in its twelve-inch pasta bowl,
it cries out for its mama. Milk in blue flasks.
   Riots of mixed beans, onions, carrots, corn
and little green broccoli trees nodding to themselves

near lettuce skirts—not to mention

the long white gravy boats that ply the tablecloth,

the whipped-up potatoes, Bombay curries, Chinese dumplings,

a rice heap in the shape of Mount Fuji,

so many sauces, so much done to chicken

I can never keep track. *The Lord is my Shepherd,*

I shall not want. And outside this house,

the howling shapes and floating eyes of my enemies

gaunt as wishes, diseased as withered hands

trying to grasp plum pudding through the air.

BUTTERING THE BREAD

How well he buttered it, from right to left
Or left to right, depending on
   The kind of bread he buttered and
Sometimes he buttered up and sometimes down.

Spoon bread, oat bread, low in fat,
High in carbohydrates, seven-grained,
   Yeasty, crusty, seeded, sliced,
No buttering was quite the same.

Johnny Cake and Mandlebrot,
Rye bread, black bread, sour dough,
   He left no bread unbuttered. Every slice
Glistened with a yellow glow.

He always knew which side to butter,
When to edge, to swirl, to slide ahead,
   Exactly how to spread it thick or thin,
Who loved to butter more than he loved bread.

And once I even saw him buttering
Both sides at once—a greasy treat
   I've never seen again—performed
On pumpernickel. Or it might have been whole wheat.

60

e

Frightening, isn't it? The alphabet's fifth letter
and most popular vowel
blown up to look like a severely damaged acorn
or an upside down baby carriage with no wheels,
or a crescent moon & baseball cap worn backward,
its saying an abbreviated shriek,
the way it spits out a dash to e-anchor itself
smack at the start of this e-century
or is like a child's drawing of a happy fish
about to gobble up anything that comes after.

HUMBLE PIE

The heart's not so awful,
   the liver, the kidneys,
and certain intestines
   boiled until tender,

mixed up with suet,
   apples and currants,
sugar and nutmeg,
   mace, clove and ginger,

then all crusted over
   with flour and water,
baked until steaming
   juices start flowing.

It's better than crow
   and goes down your gullet
smoother than rue
   or greasy good mornings.

I gulp it for breakfast,
   I chew it for lunch,
I gnaw it for supper
   and it doesn't seem much

different than being
  confirmed of my place
at the end of the table
  where no one hears grace.

Lungs and blood vessels,
  offal and spice,
one hurt, then another,
  slice after slice.

A CAUTIONARY

How do you get through this life
with its broken keyboards, its green awnings in the rain,
a battered tree top and a broken knife?
(the old man complained).
You walk a little. You stop. You hurt.
And then you go on.

Why was there nothing, and then something
and here became ocean and there became plain.
And what can we do about everything?
(the young girl asked, performing a curtsy).
You walk a little. You stop. You hurt.
And then you go on.

What if he or she dies? What if she or he dies?
If you can't trust even a Presbyterian
who will water the zinnias? Who will rack up the skies?
(questioned the woman wringing her hands).
You walk a little. You stop. You hurt.
And then you go on.

Do you know the way to San Jose? What tripped up Sisyphus?
Who took the noodles from my Ramen soup and when
were you going to tell me? Can I survive all this?
(said the madman, a gun to his head).

You walk a little. You stop. You hurt.
And then you go on.

Isn't this nonsense? Isn't advice
a joke in the ear, a clot on the brain?
One lie to another, just to be nice
(sneered the face in the crowd who once had my name).
You walk a little. You stop. You hurt.
And then you go on.

65

CRAB APPLES

Wormy and ripe, they drop
Beneath our backyard tree
Like stored-up complaints, too petty
To keep on raking up.

So maybe this is the year
We'll not bother with them—
Sour fruit, dull skin, bent stem,
We'll just leave them lying there

To rot well into Spring
And then, if they're walked upon,
They'll split and pulp, seedlings gone,
No secret they've kept worth keeping.

"*There are some things which cannot be learned quickly, and time, which is all we have, must be paid heavily for their acquiring. They are the very simplest things, and because it takes a man's life to know them, the little new that each man gets from life is very costly and the only heritage he has to leave.*" —Ernest Hemingway, *Death in the Afternoon*

"SO, WHAT DID YOU DO WITH YOUR LIFE?"

The highlight of my parents' life was seeing Al Jolson
on stage in New York.

Then, without subway money,
they walked on ten thousand clouds back to their hotel.

  as for me

I ate toast, tomato and mayonnaise sandwiches,
and kicked pebbles into the dark.

At night, I listened to dogs barking from far away,
wolves, train whistles, loons, owls, tambourines, moonlit carnivals.

I puffed my breath against a winter windowpane
and drew eyes on my ghost.

Under a flagpole, in a patch of lily-of-the-valley,
I counted, one morning, 529 white bells—each tiny as a fingertip.

Do you know how many times I've plucked daisy petals,
trying to judge love?

I was a student of blue: cobalt blue, Klein blue, turquoise blue,
blues in the night, blue indigo.

These are some smells I liked: raspberry JELL-O, skunk cabbage,
burning tire rubber, old cellars with high grimy windows.

The most beautiful motion in the world, I thought,
was the canoeing J-stroke: pull, twist the wrist, feather, dip, and pull again.

It seemed like writing a line of poetry:
pull, twist the wrist, feather, dip, and pull again.

or living through the ages:
pull, twist the wrist, feather, dip, and pull again.

I wore cheap wristwatches, always with black leather bands,
and my wallet in my right hip pocket.

I made out so many lists,
some days I forgot myself, or I crossed myself out.

I touched mossy stones under water. I spent days
trying to levitate, foolish as that sounds.

When I was sixty-two, I bought a small ceramic bird
that filled one hand, as if my hand was a nest.

And a miniature Chinese-red box shaped like a river barge
to float upon a bookcase and place coins and spices in.

PIXELS

Each small thing he examines, every microdot
in the computer's blown-up photograph
of rose petals, thumbnails, many portions
of wide and narrow letters (without a microscope
to take him further in)
blurs and fades to white or gray or dark
from which, at last, he pulls his eyes away,
blinking and tearing. It's then he understands why
before Galileo
the world seemed details that mysteriously
formed out of the void, and the void to elements:
from air, the cedar branch
drifting over Huan Valley; from fire,
iron parapets and sibyl's smoke; from water
the wondrous scales of many fish; and from the earth,
green meadows running on and on
until stopped by forest. He taps some keys
and the picture shrinks, resolves itself
into the small scene that he started with,
the woman pressing a flower in between torn pages
of a book so thin it must be poetry.

ON TENTERHOOKS

Suspense seldom kills, but too often
stretched between the hooks, the cloth
drying in the sun so its weave might be straightened
rips in one section and the whole taut fabric,
so like a riveted drumskin or the canvas of a trampoline,
goes slack, its practical use over—
that anxiety which kept us searching the heavens,
wringing our hands, wiping our brows,
questioning the outcome,
only a matter of tension: that intangible
way of holding things we'd just as soon let go.

I WILL BUY A CHICKEN: A DUET

—after three sentences on simplifying life
from Paul Theroux's The Pillars of Hercules

I will buy a chicken. *I will drink some water.*
I will play some music for the people of the town.
I will read a comic book for laughter.
I will watch an elevator moving up and down.

I will finger neckties. I will count to ten.
I will light a candle in the church.
I will throw some pebbles at the ocean.
I will touch the leaves of that white birch.

I will see the streetlights going on and off.
I will sing a tune my mother sang.
I will hear red motorcycles cough.
I will taste the bubbles in meringue.

I will pet a dog, a cat, a tree, a stone.
I will shuffle cards. I will wish some wishes.
I will look into the bottom of an ice cream cone.
I will make some beds. *I will break some dishes.*

I will whisper secrets to a rusty statue.
I will shrug my shoulders. I will swing my arms.
I will smell the insides of a running shoe.
I will suck the color out of Lucky Charms.

I will choose a wayside. I will eat a breadstick.

I will shout "God help us!" when the morning's almost done.

I will give a soda can a soccer kick.

I will sink my teeth into the ankle of the sun.

B & B

Are you so tired then, Stranger? Are you so tired
that you can't lift your arms above a whisper
or extend your hand?
Are you so tired that you accept the verdicts of salamanders
and fish bones, and the sun in the morning and the moon at night,
so tired that you think another day's another day
and nothing in your life is new—while all around you
ideas percolate, branches break, computers go wild? Stranger,
                    are you so tired
that you'd give up wishing for a second chance
if you could only have a day or two in the country,
sitting in an Adirondack chair with your wristwatch off
until someone calls, "Croquet, croquet. Anyone for croquet?"
Are you tired enough to not care who's invading who,
who's playing who, who speaks for who, who's rising to the top,
whose cat's got whose tongue?
Was it experiences with an early grave that did you in?
Why do you always think of yourself as half-dissolved,
wretchedly torn? Talk to us, Stranger,
tell us what we've forgotten about room dividers,
bottle caps, memory lapse, cufflinks, sad sacks,
and how young men/young women stand on various fire escapes
promising themselves the world
but at the same time sensing they'll be lost in money,
houses and children. Stranger, are you tired enough

to lay down your burdens, to think of opportunities
finally as things to let slip by with no regrets,
like early morning starlings rising above green pastures,
skimming across bristlegrass and wildflowers,
heading somewhere no one knows? If so,
we'll straighten the pictures on our guest room walls,
turn down the covers, fluff up the pillows.... Tap at our door.
              Stranger,
or send us your message on the Internet's blue waves,
and we'll provide for you a place to rest your head.

DON'T TELL ME THERE'S NO HOPE

The Future could be wrong. For all I know,
it could be a bowl of unripe strawberries
or a cell phone ringing to itself in an empty room,
or that mysterious Asian saying,
"A day without vegetables is like a day without vegetables."
Step into the wrong Future
and you're likely to find yourself humming Rascal Flatts
on the sidewalks of New York. The wrong Future
could be a blinking smoke detector light on a motel ceiling,
a town where roosters crow in the distance,
some preacher saying, *"From everywhere,*
God rushes toward you." Yet for all I know,
that Future's already rented out to someone else
who can walk where I can only see:
Here's to you, wrong Future! ... I wanted
a life simple as reading the wind,
roads with nothing on them but me and an occasional Fed Ex truck,
but what I got was another gedanken experiment,
delays, false hopes, mournful harmonica music.
So here's to all the wrong paths I'm about to take,
the wrong people I'll race or stumble off with,
all my wrong-headed visions.
Here's to salt water taffy, power lines, cross-purposes,
that sign by the Colorado meadow: *Wildflowers in Progress,*
how, near the end of a perfect set, the lead-guitarist says,

> *"Let's take it on home"*
and everything falls into place, the audience may weep,
the houselights stay dim for minutes afterward,
then hands find each other, the way they always do.

"SEE THE PYRAMIDS ALONG THE NILE"

I'll not be doing that now, nor the tropical islands,
the Algerian marketplace, the sunrise, the ocean.
Too many years vanished. I'll be in a cottage by a lake,
stumbling through books with pages missing,
looking from doorways at my nondescript back yard.
But Godspeed those who still wander,
Godspeed the great lovers, the great adventurers,
the movies and statues they'll become,
lonesome and blue.... Here, this evening,
everything will be quiet except my neighbor's buzzsaw
cutting into even lengths the wood
he'll use for something or other that he doesn't need...
and all I didn't do or dare to do,
will haunt me—those dreams appearing elsewhere,
the jungle wet with rain,
you who I never met, arms lifted up into another's arms,
in a small house in Cairo, in a market stall
with the abacus and the veils,
or three rows ahead, your face tucked toward the window,
when I belonged to no one on that silver plane.

"AND ALL SHALL BE WELL; AND ALL SHALL BE WELL; AND ALL MANNER OF THING SHALL BE WELL"

And you shall be lost in tinker toys and spices.
And alongside the garden walls of old computers,
women will walk in long pale dresses, scattering roses,
men shall lie down beside their work,
arms thrown across it.
And all shall be well. And the sins of our fathers
shall be as boulders and fruit flies on an Idaho morning.
You shall read Yeats' poems
in lieu of prayer, whispering the lines
as quietly as you might paint each raindrop
in a landscape of cedars or a watercolor of plum blossoms.
And all shall be well. And evil
will blow itself up a thousand miles from Darfur
with no one to pronounce "Ginnie Mae" or "Rumplestiltskin"
or "Martyr, Martyr, ring around the martyr."
You shall not fear, you shall confound the world
with absolute kindness and forgiveness,
and with the right ear of a turkey in the straw,
and one of those 120-count boxes of Crayola crayons:
Bittersweet, Cornflower, Maize,
Periwinkle, Prussian Blue,
Thistle, Sunglow, Denim,
Timberwolf, Tumbleweed, Fern,

80

Outer Space, Shadow.

And as did the Harmoniums in the Caves of Mercury,

you shall recite, *"Here I am. Here I am. Here I am."*

And you shall be answered,

"So glad you are. So glad you are. So glad you are."

And you shall gaze upon a hazelnut

and know that in the palm of your hand

is all that is made

and you are created, you are loved, you are sustained

by iambs and anapests, by Julian of Norwich,

by the black and white chickadee that just now came to my window.

And despite insult and spittle and disfiguring and bruising and lingering pain,

all shall be well;

and all manner of thing shall be well.

The Author

Dick Allen has received poetry writing fellowships from the National
Endowment for the Arts and the Ingram Merrill Foundation, as well as the
Robert Frost Prize for Poetry and The Hart Crane Poetry Prize. His books
include *The Day Before, Ode to the Cold War: Poems New and Selected,
Flight and Pursuit, Overnight in the Guest House of the Mystic,* and *Regions
with No Proper Names,* among others. His poems have been selected for *The
Best American Poetry* volumes of 1991, 1994, 1998, 1999, and 2006.

Jon Gordon